PIANO/VOCAL/GUITAR

ROCK 'N' ROLL
100 OF THE BEST

P9-DBO-563

In the history of rock 'n' roll, the years spanning 1954 through 1965 were some of the most musically exciting. The raw energy of rock which was so evident in its early years seemed to resurge in the early 60's, with the Beatles leading the invasion of British talent to American shores. This collection brings together 100 of the biggest hits from that era, hits which were performed by such legendary artists as Elvis, Jerry Lee Lewis, Chuck Berry, Brenda Lee, the Coasters and Buddy Holly. Rock 'n' roll is truly here to stay, and we hope that you enjoy this anthology of the songs and artists who helped make it an American musical success story.

HAL LEONARD
PUBLISHING
CORPORATION

Home Office: National Sales Office:
960 East Mark Street   8112 West Bluemound Road
Winona MN 55987   Milwaukee WI 53213

CONTENTS

ALL SHOOK UP

Medium Shuffle Rhythm

Words and Music by OTIS BLACKWELL
and ELVIS PRESLEY

A - well - a, bless my soul,__ What's wrong with me?__ I'm itch - ing like a man__ on a

fuz - zy tree__ My friends say I'm act - in' queer as a bug__ I'm in love I'm

all shook up!__ Mm - mm oh, oh, yeah,__ yeah! _____ My

hands are sha-ky and my knees are weak.___ I can't seem to stand___ on my

own two feet,___ Who do you thank when you have such luck?___ I'm in

Eb7   F7

love! I'm all shook up!___ Mm___ mm oh, oh, yeah,___

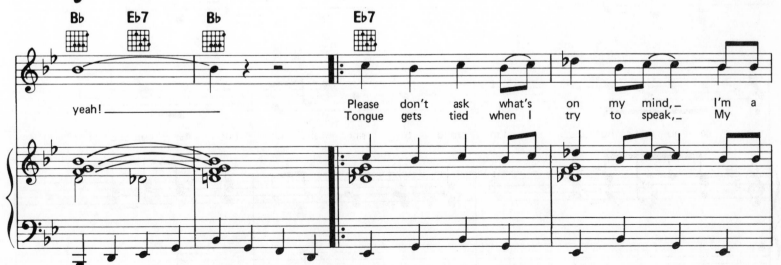

Bb Eb7 Bb   Eb7

yeah!_____

Please don't ask what's on my mind,___ I'm a
Tongue gets tied when I try to speak,___ My

ALONG CAME JONES

Words and Music by JERRY LEIBER
and MIKE STOLLER

Moderately Bright

BACK IN THE U.S.A.

Words and Music by CHUCK BERRY

Medium beat

1. Oh, well, oh, well, I feel so good to-day,

We just touched ground on an in-ter-na-tional run-way. ___ Jet pro-

pelled back home, from o-ver-seas to the U. S. A. ___ 2. New York, Los An-gel-es, (4.)

oh, how I yearned for you,   De-troit, Chi-ca-go, Chat-ta-noo-ga, Bat-on

Rouge.   Let a-lone just to be   at my home back in ol' St. Lou.

D.S. al Coda   ⊕ CODA

3. Did   Lou.   6. Well

5. (Instrumental)

3. Did I miss the skyscrapers, did I miss the long freeway?
   From the coast of California to the shores of the Delaware Bay.
   You can bet your life I did, till I got back to the U. S. A.

4. Looking hard for a drive-in, searching for a corner café,
   Where hamburgers sizzle on an open grill night and day,
   Yeah, and a juke-box jumping with records like in the U. S. A.

5. *Instrumental*

6. Well, I'm so glad I'm livin' in the U. S. A.,
   Yes, I'm so glad I'm livin' in the U. S. A.,
   Anything you want, we got it right here in the U. S. A.

AT THE HOP

Words and Music by ARTHUR SINGER,
JOHN MEDORA and DAVID WHITE

BANDSTAND BOOGIE

Words by BARRY MANILOW
and BRUCE SUSSMAN
Music by CHARLES ALBERTINE

We're go - in' hop - pin', *(Hop!)* we're go - in' hop - pin' to - day, where things are
swing - in', *(Swing!)* we're gon - na swing in the crowd, and we'll be

pop - pin' *(Pop!)* the Phil - a - del - phi - a way; we're gon - na drop in *(Drop!)* on all the
cling - in' *(Cling!)* and float - in' high on a cloud, the phones are ring - in' *(Ring!)* my mom and

Stroll on A - mer - i - can, Lin - dy Hop and Slop, it's A - mer - i - can

Eb9   D7+5   Db13   C7   Bmaj7

tune in, I'm on, turn on, I'm in, I'm on!

Bb6   Eb9   Eb/F

To - day,

C7   Bmaj7   Bb6

Band - stand.

BIRD DOG

By BOUDLEAUX BRYANT

VERSE

Johnny is a jok-er Spoken: (He's a bird) A ver-y fun-ny jok-er

(He's a bird) But when he jokes my hon-ey (He's a dog) His

jok-in' ain't so fun-ny (What a dog) John-ny is the jok-er that's a-

C7 G D7 G7
try - in' to steal my ba - by (He's a bird dog)
CHORUS
C7 G
Hey, bird dog, get a - way from my quail. Hey, bird dog, you're on
D7 C7
the wrong trail. Bird dog, you'd bet - ter leave my lov - ey dove a lone.
G G7 C7
Hey, bird dog, get a - way from my chick

Hey, bird dog, you'd bet-ter get a-way quick.___ Bird dog, you'd bet-ter find a

chick-en lit-tle of your own.___

own.___

VERSE 2. Johnny sings a love song *(Like a bird)*
He sings the sweetest love song *(You ever heard)*
But when he sings to my gal *(What a howl)*
To me he's just a wolf dog *(On the prowl)*
Johnny wants to fly away and puppy love my baby *(He's a bird dog)*
(CHORUS)

3. Johnny kissed the teacher *(He's a bird)*
He tiptoed up to reach her *(He's a bird)*
Well, he's the teacher's pet now *(He's a dog)*
What he wants he can get now *(What a dog)*
He even made the teacher let him sit next to my baby. *(He's a bird dog)*
(CHORUS)

BLUE SUEDE SHOES

Words and Music by CARL LEE PERKINS

Bright Tempo (not too fast)

Chorus

Well, it's one for the mon-ey, two for the show,

three to get read-y, now go, cat, go But don't you

BLUEBERRY HILL

Words and Music by
AL LEWIS, LARRY STOCK and VINCENT ROSE

Moderately

BO DIDDLEY

Brightly *(a la Calypso)*

Words and Music by ELLAS McDANIEL

Bo Did-dley'll buy ba-by a dia-mond ring,

If that dia-mond ring don't shine,—

He's gon-na take it to a pri-vate eye.

To make his pret-ty ba-by a Sun-day hat.

Won't you come to my house and rack that bone,

Take my ba-by all the way from home.

Look at that bo-do, Oh,

where's he been, ___

Up to your house and gone a-gain.

Bo Did-dl-ey, Bo Did-dl-ey, have you heard, ___

Repeat and Fade

My ___ pret-ty ba-by said she was a bird.

BOOK OF LOVE

Words and Music by WARREN DAVIS,
GEORGE MALONE and CHARLES PATRICK

BREAD AND BUTTER

By J. Turnbow
and L. Parks

Moderate Rock Beat

I like bread and but - ter   I like toast and jam

That's what my ba - by   feeds___ me   I'm her lov - in'   man

2. She don't cook mashed potatoes
   Don't cook T-bone steak
   Don't feed me peanut butter
   She knows that I can't take
   No more bread and butter
   No more toast and jam
   He found his baby eatin'
   With some other man

3. Got home early one mornin'
   Much to my surprise
   She was eatin' chicken and dumplins
   With some other guy
   No more bread and butter
   No more toast and jam
   I found my baby eatin'
   With some other man

BYE BYE, LOVE

Words and Music by FELICE BRYANT
and BOUDLEAUX BRYANT

Moderately fast

There goes my ba - by___ with some - one new;___ She sure looks
ro - mance,___ I'm through with love___ I'm through with

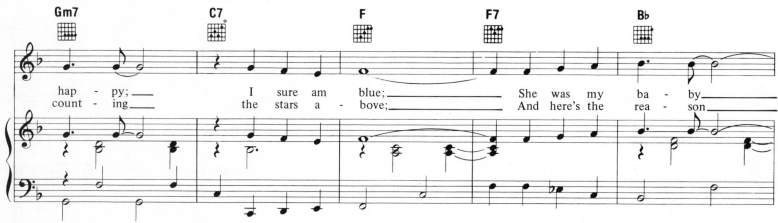

hap - py;___ I sure am blue;___ She was my ba - by___
count - ing___ the stars a - bove;___ And here's the rea - son___

till he stepped in;___ Good - bye to ro - mance___
that I'm so free;___ My lo - vin' ba - by___

C.C. RIDER

Words and Music by CHUCK WILLIS

BUT I DO

Words and Music by ROBERT C. GUIDRY
and PAUL GAYTEN

I don't know why I love you but I do. ___
can't sleep nights be - cause I feel so rest - less,

don't know why I cry so, but I do. ___
don't know what to do, I feel so help - less.
And

on - ly know I'm lone - ly and that I want you on - ly,
since you've been a - way. ___ I cry both night and day, ___
I

CHANTILLY LACE

Moderate Boogie Woogie

Words and Music by J.P. RICHARDSON

CHARLIE BROWN

Words and Music by JERRY LEIBER
and MIKE STOLLER

Medium Bright Rock

Lyrics:

Fee fee fi fi fo fo fum; I smell smoke in the au-di-to-ri-um. Char-lie

Brown, Char-lie Brown, he's a clown, that Char-lie Brown. He's

gon-na get caught, just you wait and see. *Spoken: "Why is ev-'ry-bod-y al-ways pick-in' on me?"* That's

Guitar Tacet

him on his knees; I know that's him,_ yell-ing, "Sev-en come e-lev-en" down in the boys'_ gym. Char-lie

Bb7

F

Brown, Char-lie Brown, he's a clown, that Char-lie Brown. He's

C7

Bb7

F Guitar Tacet

gon-na get caught, just you wait and see. *Spoken:"Why is ev-'ry-bod-y al-ways pick-in' on me?"*

Bb

Ab

Who's al-ways writ-ing on the walls? Who's al-ways goof-ing in the halls?

54

COME GO WITH ME

Words and Music by C.E. QUICK

Slow beat

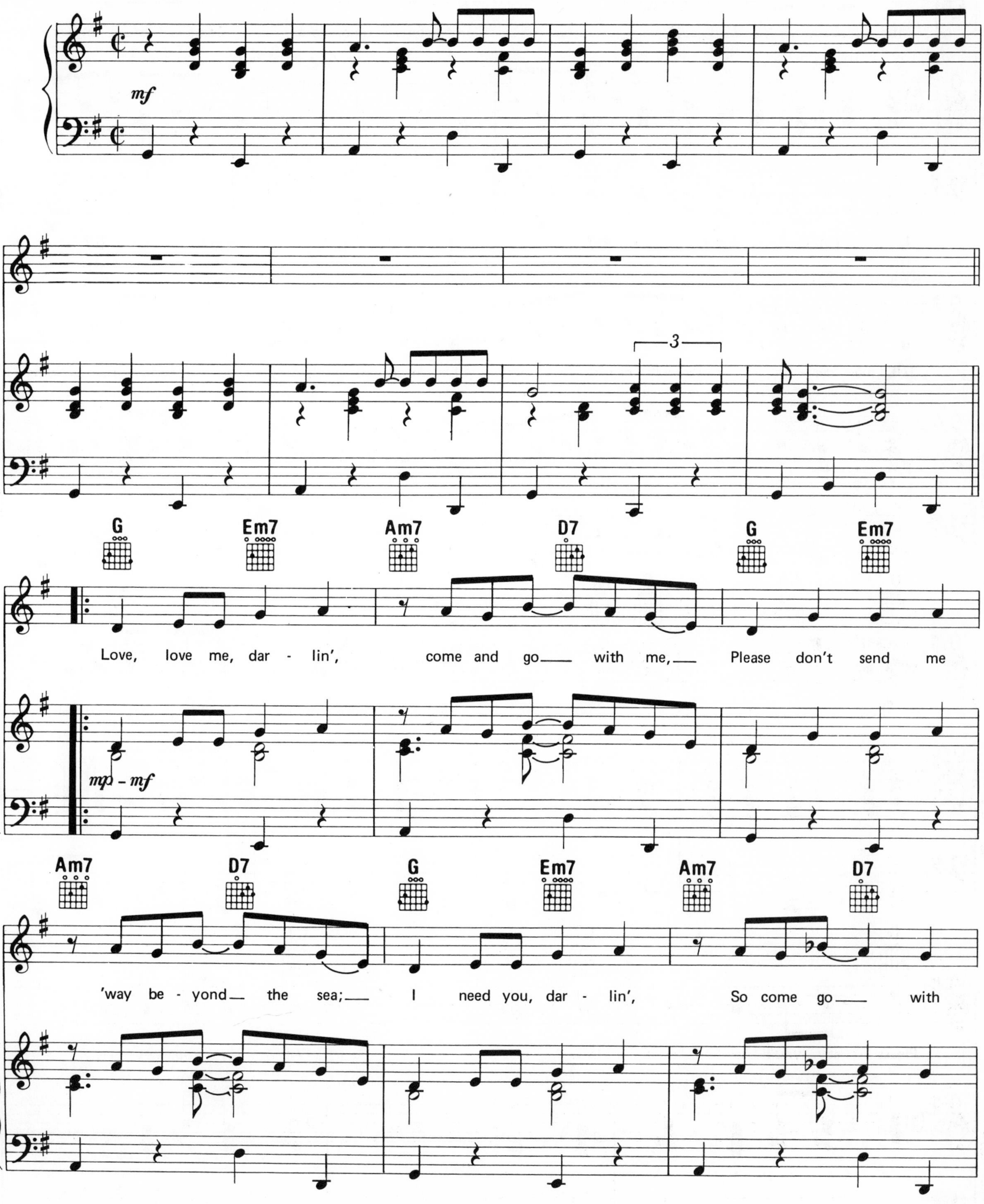

mf
3
G
Em7
Am7
D7
G
Em7
mp - mf
Love, love me, dar - lin', come and go with me, Please don't send me
Am7
D7
G
Em7
Am7
D7
'way be - yond the sea; I need you, dar - lin', So come go with

DADDY COOL

Words and Music by FRANK C. SLAY, JR.,
and BOB CREWE

DON'T BE CRUEL
(To A Heart That's True)

Words and Music by OTIS BLACKWELL
and ELVIS PRESLEY

DIANA

Words and Music by PAUL ANKA

DUKE OF EARL

Moderately with a rock beat

Words and Music by EARL EDWARDS,
EUGENE DIXON and BERNICE WILLIAMS

EARTH ANGEL

Slowly with a beat

Words and Music by DOOTSIE WILLIAMS

FOR YOUR PRECIOUS LOVE

Words and Music by ARTHUR BROOKS,
RICHARD BROOKS and JERRY BUTLER

HIS LATEST FLAME

Words and Music by DOC POMUS
and MORT SHUMAN

GREAT BALLS OF FIRE

Words and Music by OTIS BLACKWELL
and JACK HAMMER

Bright Rock Tempo

You shake my nerves and you rat-tle my brain___ Too much love drives a

man in-sane.___ You broke my will, but what a thrill.

Good-ness gra-cious, great___ balls of fi-re! I laughed at love 'cause I

HALLELUJAH I LOVE HER SO

Words and Music by RAY CHARLES

HEARTBEAT

Words and Music by BOB MONTGOMERY
and NORMAN PETTY

With an easy flow

Heart - beat, _____ why do you miss when_ my ba - by kiss - es me?
Heart - beat, _____ why do you skip when_ my ba - by's lips_meet mine?

Heart - beat, _____ why does a love kiss_stay
Heart - beat, _____ why do you flip, then_give

in my mem - o - ry?
me a skip - beat sign?

HELLO MARY LOU
(GOODBYE HEART)

Words and Music by CAVET MANGIARACINA
and GENE PITNEY

Moderately

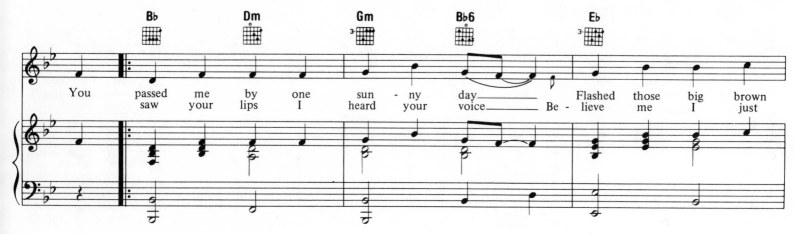

You passed me by one sun - ny day____ Flashed those big brown
saw your lips I heard your voice____ Be - lieve me I just

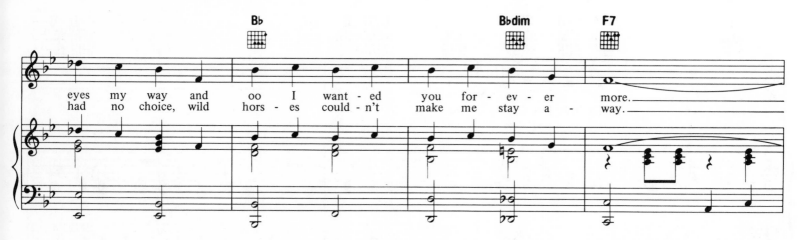

eyes my way and oo I want - ed you for - ev - er more.____
had no choice, wild hors - es could - n't make me stay a - way.____

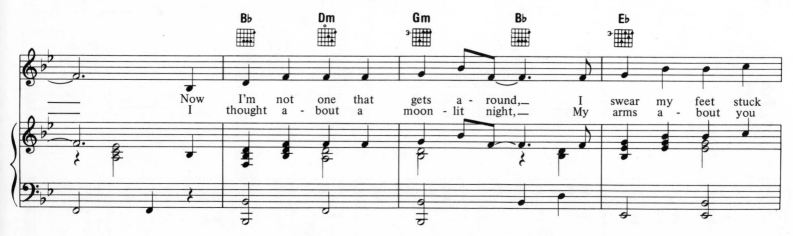

I Now I'm not one that gets a - round,____ I swear my feet stuck
thought a - bout a moon - lit night,____ My arms a - bout you

HI-HEEL SNEAKERS

With a beat

Words and Music by ROBERT HIGGENBOTHAM

HOUND DOG

Words and Music by JERRY LEIBER
and MIKE STOLLER

Medium Rock

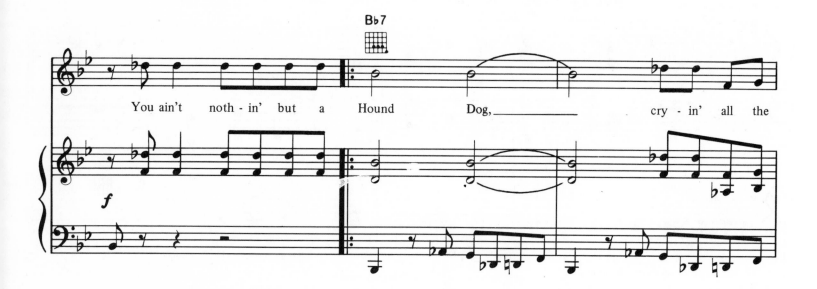

You ain't noth - in' but a Hound Dog, _____ cry - in' all the

time. You ain't noth - in' but a Hound Dog, _____

I ONLY WANT TO BE WITH YOU

Words and Music by MIKE HAWKER
and IVOR RAYMONDE

Moderately

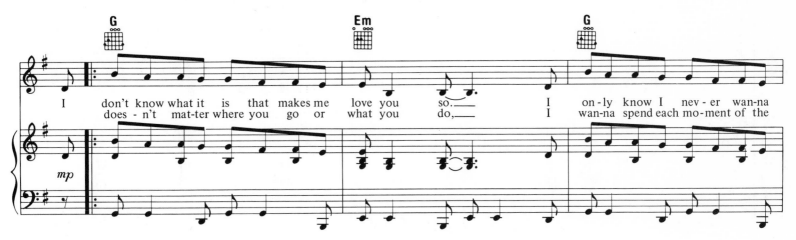

I don't know what it is that makes me love you so. I on-ly know I nev-er wan-na
does-n't mat-ter where you go or what you do, I wan-na spend each mo-ment of the

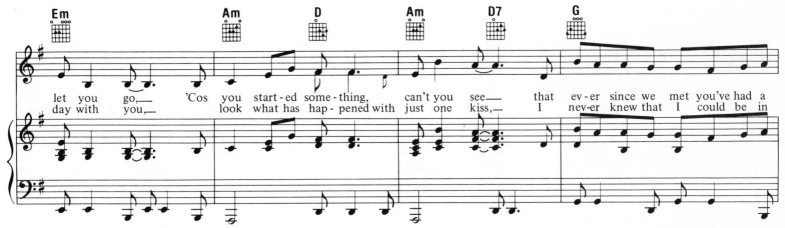

let you go, 'Cos you start-ed some-thing, can't you see that ev-er since we met you've had a
day with you, look what has hap-pened with just one kiss, I nev-er knew that I could be in

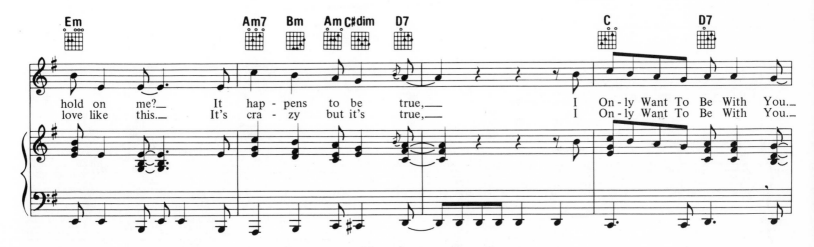

hold on me? It hap-pens to be true, I On-ly Want To Be With You.
love like this. It's cra-zy but it's true, I On-ly Want To Be With You.

I FOUGHT THE LAW

By S. CURTIS

I SAW HER STANDING THERE

Words and Music by JOHN LENNON
and PAUL McCARTNEY

Moderately bright

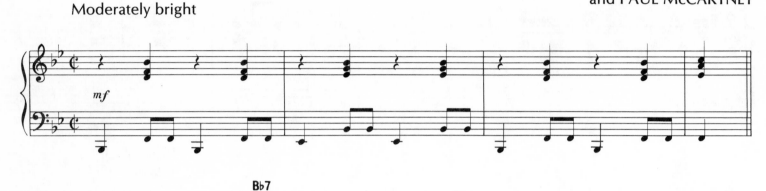

Well, she was just sev-en-teen, And you
she looked at me, And

know what I mean, And the way she looked was
I, I could see that be-fore too long, I'd

'way be-yond com-pare. So how could I
fall in love with her. She would-n't

Eb   Gb   Bb

dance with an - oth-er,____ Oh, when I saw her
dance with an - oth-er,____ Oh, when I saw her

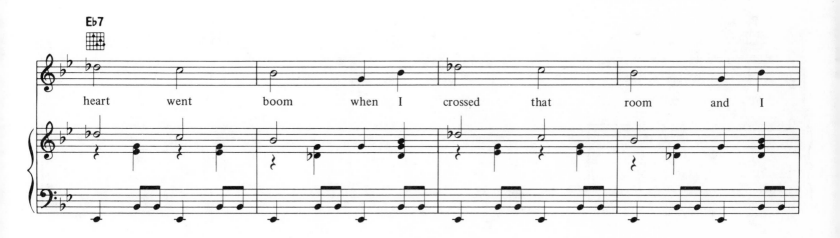

F7   F+   Bb

stand - ing there.   Well,
stand - ing there.   Well, my

Eb7

heart went boom when I crossed that room and I

F7

held her hand in mine.____   Well, we

danced through the night,___ And we held each oth-er tight,___ And be-

fore too long,___ I fell in love with her.___ Now

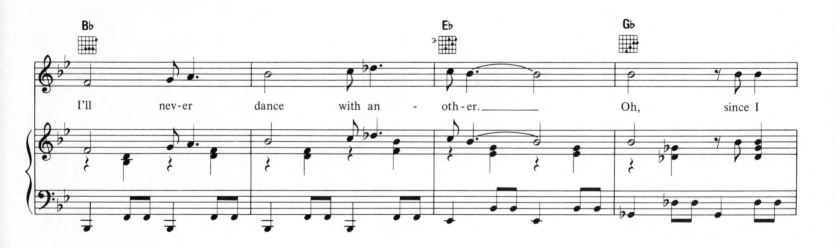

I'll nev-er dance with an - oth-er.___ Oh, since I

saw her stand - ing there.___

JAILHOUSE ROCK

Words and Music by JERRY LEIBER
and MIKE STOLLER

Medium Rock

1. The war-den threw a par-ty in the coun-ty jail.___ The
2. ___ Spi-der Mur-phy played the ten-or sax-o-phone.___
3. ___ Num-ber For-ty-sev-en said to Num-ber Three:___ ___

pris-on band was there and they be-gan to wail.___ The
Lit-tle Joe was blow-in' on the slide trom-bone.___ The
You're the cut-est jail-bird I___ ev-er did see.___ I

4. The sad sack was a-sittin' on a block of stone,
   Way over in the corner weeping all alone.
   The warden said: Hey, buddy, don't you be no square.
   If you can't find a partner, use a wooden chair!
   Let's rock, etc.

5. Shifty Henry said to Bugs: For Heaven's sake,
   No one's lookin'; now's our chance to make a break.
   Bugsy turned to Shifty and he said: Nix, nix;
   I wanna stick around a while and get my kicks,
   Let's rock, etc.

I WANT TO HOLD YOUR HAND

Words and Music by JOHN LENNON
and PAUL McCARTNEY

With a beat

Oh yeh, I'll_____ tell you some - thing I think you'll un - der -

stand. Then I'll_____ say that some - thing,

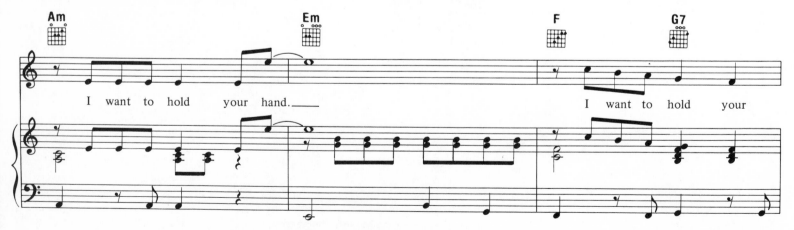

I want to hold your hand.____ I want to hold your

hand,_____ I want to hold your hand, and when I

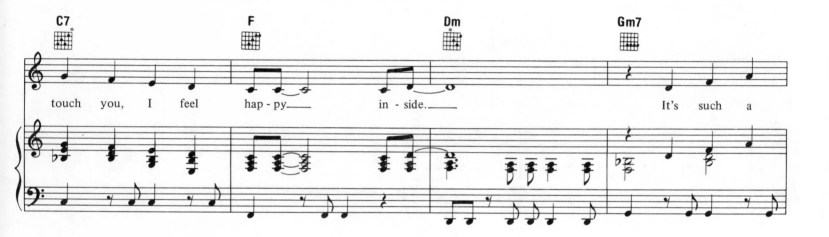

touch you, I feel hap-py_____ in-side.____ It's such a

feel-ing that my love I can't hide,____ I can't hide,____ I can't hide._

_____ Yeh, you_____ got that some-thing,

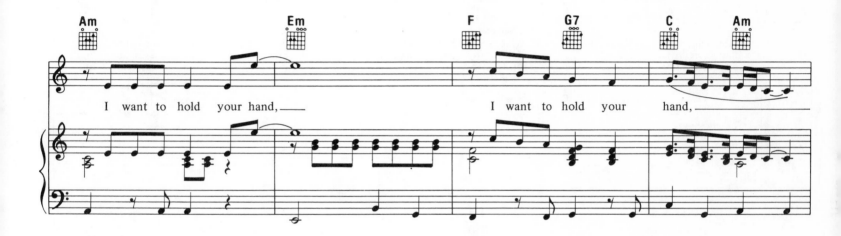

I'M LOOKING FOR SOMEONE TO LOVE

Words and Music by BUDDY HOLLY
and NORMAN PETTY

I'M SORRY

Words and Music by RONNIE SELF
and DUB ALBRITTEN

IT'S MY PARTY

Words and Music by HERB WIENER,
WALLY GOLD and JOHN GLUCK, JR.

Moderately bright

No - bod - y knows___ where my John - ny has gone,___ "But
Play all my rec - ords, keep danc - ing all night,___ But
Ju - dy and John - ny just walked thru the door,___ But

Ju - dy left___ the same time.
leave me a - lone___ for a - while,
Like a queen___ with her king,

Why was he
'Til John - ny's
Oh, what a

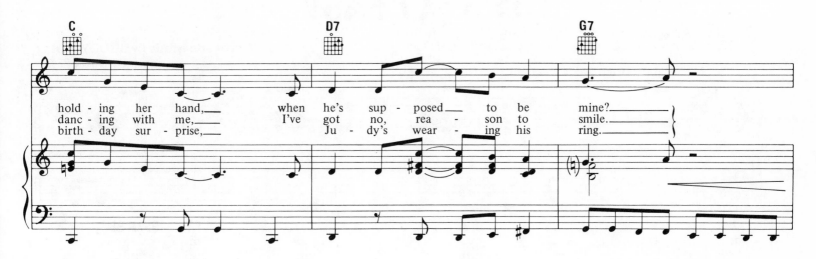

hold - ing her hand,____ when he's sup - posed____ to be mine?____
danc - ing with me,____ I've got no, rea - son to smile.____
birth - day sur - prise,____ Ju - dy's wear - ing his ring.____

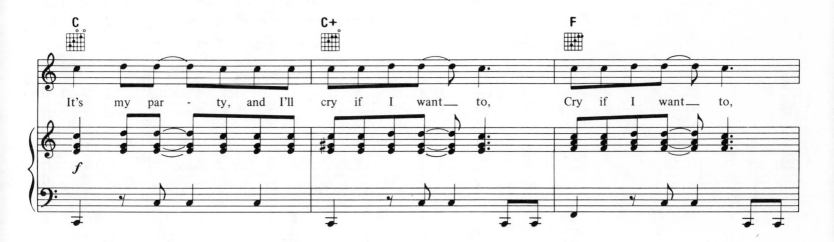

It's my par - ty, and I'll cry if I want____ to, Cry if I want____ to,

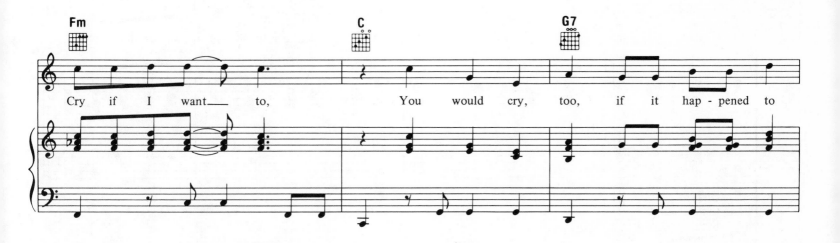

Cry if I want____ to, You would cry, too, if it hap - pened to

you.

IT'S SO EASY

Words and Music by BUDDY HOLLY
and NORMAN PETTY

It's so eas-y to fall in love,___ It's so eas-y to___ fall___ in love.___

Peo-ple tell me love's for fools,_ So here I go___ break-ing all of the rules___

It seems so eas-y, (Hum),_____ so dog-gone eas-y;

JOHNNY B. GOODE

Words and Music by CHUCK BERRY

Deep down in Lou-'si-an - a, close to New Or - leans,___ Way back up in the woods a - mong the
car - ry his gui - tar___ in a gun - ny sack,___ Go sit be - neath the tree___ by the
moth - er told him, "Some-day you will be a man___ And you will be the lead - er of a

ev - er - greens;___ There stood an old___ cab - in made of earth and wood,___ Where
rail - road track;___ Ol' en - gi - neer in the train___ sit - tin' in the shade,___ Where
big old band;___ Man - y peo - ple com - in' from___ miles a - round,___ To

lived a coun - try boy___ named___ John - ny B. Goode.___ Who'd nev - er ev - er learned to read or
Strum-min' with the rhy-thm that the driv - ers made.___ The peo - ple pass - in' by,___ they would
hear you play your mu - sic till the sun goes down.___ May - be some day your name - 'll be in

THE LION SLEEPS TONIGHT
(WIMOWEH) (MBUBE)

New lyric and revised music by HUGO PERETTI,
LUIGI CREATORE, GEORGE WEISS and ALBERT STANTON
Based on a song by SOLOMON LINDA and PAUL CAMPBELL

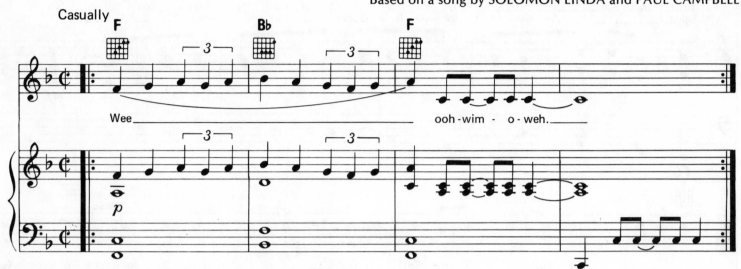

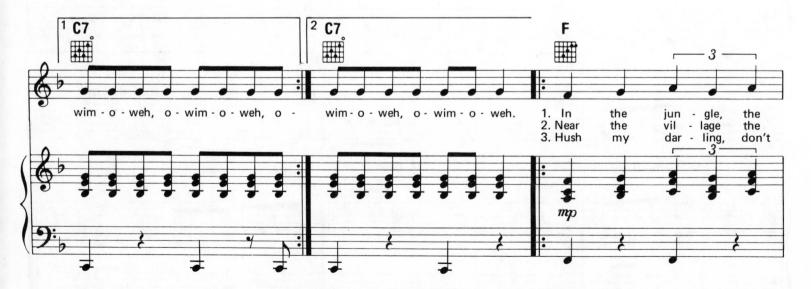

LOLLIPOP

Words and Music by BEVERLY ROSS
and JULIUS DIXON

Lol-li-pop, lol-li-pop, Oh,___ lol-li, lol-li, lol-li, lol-li-pop, lol-li-pop, Oh,___ lol-li, lol-li, lol-li, lol-li-pop, lol-li-pop, Oh,___ lol-li, lol-li, lol-li, lol-li-pop.

Call my ba-by lol-li-pop,
Cra-zy way she thrills-a me,

LIPSTICK ON YOUR COLLAR

Moderate rock beat

Words by EDNA LEWIS
Music by GEORGE GOEHRING

When you left me all a-lone at the Rec-ord Hop, Told me you were
go-in' out for a so-da pop, You were gone for quite a while,
Half an hour or more. You came back and man, Oh man, This is what I

You said it be-longed to me; Made me stop and think, Then I no-ticed
yours was red, mine was ba-by pink, You walked in but Ma-ry Jane,
Lip-stick all a mess. Were you smooch-in' my best friend? Guess the an-swer's

LONELY BOY

Words and Music by PAUL ANKA

MABELLENE

Words and Music by CHUCK BERRY,
RUSS FRATTO and ALAN FREED

Ma - bel - lene, _____ Why can't_ you be true? Oh! Ma - bel -

lene, _____ Why can't_ you be true?_____ You've

start -ed back do -in' the things you used to do._____ 1. As

LOUIE, LOUIE

Words and Music by RICHARD BERRY

Medium Rock Beat

Lou - ie, Lou - ie, Me got - ta go____

Lou - ie, Lou - ie,

Me got - ta go____

A fine lit - tle girl, she
Three nights and____ days we
Me see Ja - mai - ca

LOVE ME TENDER

Words and Music by
ELVIS PRESLEY & VERA MATSON

Moderately slow

Verse

1. Love Me Ten - der, love me sweet;
2. Love Me Ten - der, love me long;
3. Love Me Ten - der, love me dear;

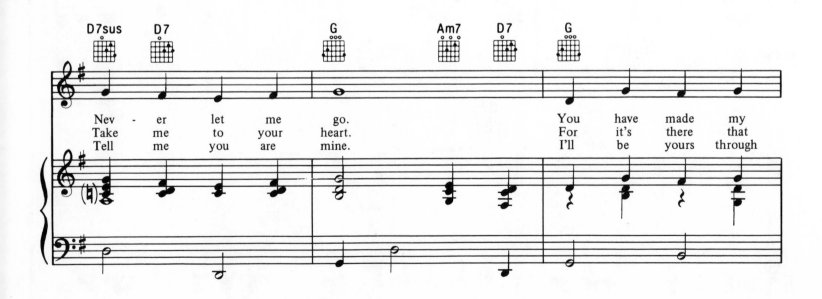

Nev - er let me go. You have made my
Take me to your heart. For it's there that
Tell me you are mine. I'll be yours through

EXTRA VERSE   4. When at last my dreams come true,
Darling, this I know:
Happiness will follow you
Everywhere you go.

MAYBE BABY

Moderate Country beat

Words and Music by NORMAN PETTY
and CHARLES HARDIN

May-be, ba-by, I'll have you.___ May-be ba-by, you'll be true.___

May-be, ba-by, I'll have you___ for me.___

It's fun-ny, hon-ey; you don't care.___ You nev-er lis-ten to my prayer.___

Instrumental

E
A
B
E
A/E
E
May-be, ba-by, you will love me some day.
Well,
A
E
you are the one that makes me sad, and you are the one that makes me glad.
A
B
E
When some-day you want me, I'll be there. Just wait and see.
May-be, ba-by,
C#m
E
C#m
E
I'll have you.
May-be, ba-by, you'll be true.
May-be, ba-by,

I'll have you___ for me.___   me.

May-be, ba-by, I'll have you.___ May-be, ba-by, you'll be true.___

Repeat and fade

May-be, ba-by, I'll have you___ for___ me.

MEMPHIS, TENNESSEE

Moderate bright tempo

Words and Music by CHUCK BERRY

Long dis-tance, in-for-ma-tion, Give me Mem-phis, Ten-nes-see;
Help me, in-for-ma-tion, Get in touch with my Ma-rie; She's the

Help me find the par-ty try-ing to get in touch with me. She
on-ly one who'd phone me here from Mem-phis Ten-nes-see. Her

could not leave her num-ber, but I know who placed the call 'cause my
home is on the south___ side,___ High up on a ridge,

Chords: C D A7 D7 A7 G A7 D

miss____ her and all the fun we had. But we were pulled a-part, be-cause her
on her cheek that trick-l'd from her eye. Ma-rie is on-ly six years old,____

Mom did not a-gree, and____ tore a-part our hap-py home in Mem-phis Ten-nes-
in-for-ma-tion, please, try to put me through to her in Mem-phis Ten-nes-

1

see.
see.

2

NOT FADE AWAY

Moderately bright

Words and Music by CHARLES HARDIN
and NORMAN PETTY

Well, I'm gon-na tell you how it's gon-na be._
My love is big-ger than a Ca-dil-lac._

You're gon-na give your lov-in' to me._
I try to love you but you drive__ me back._

love to last__ more than one day._____
Your love for me has got to be real_____

146

OH BOY!

Words and Music by SUNNY WEST,
BILL TILGHMAN and NORMAN PETTY

SUGAR SHACK

Words and Music by KEITH McCORMACK
and FAYE VOSS

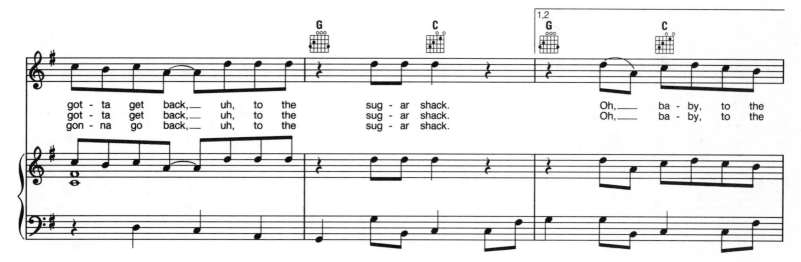

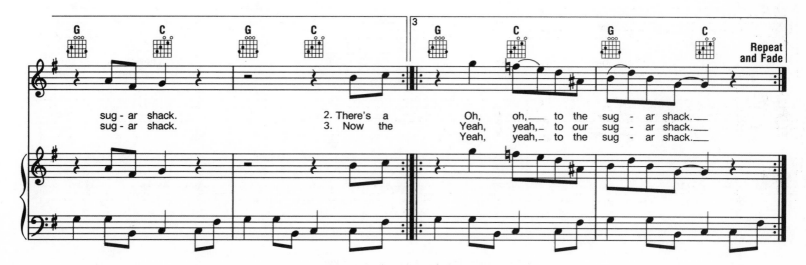

ONLY THE LONELY
(KNOW THE WAY I FEEL)

By R. ORBISON
and J. MELSON

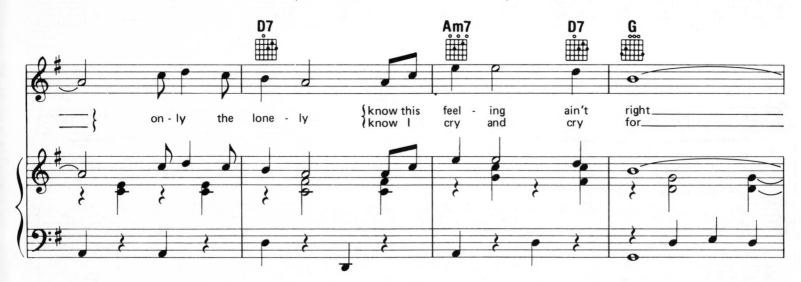

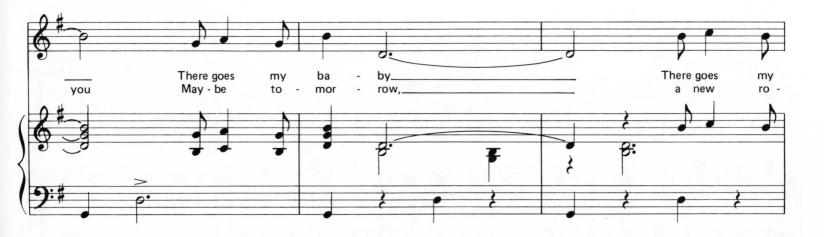

Buck Ram's
ONLY YOU
(And You Alone)

Words & Music by
BUCK RAM and ANDE RAND

Slowly, with feeling

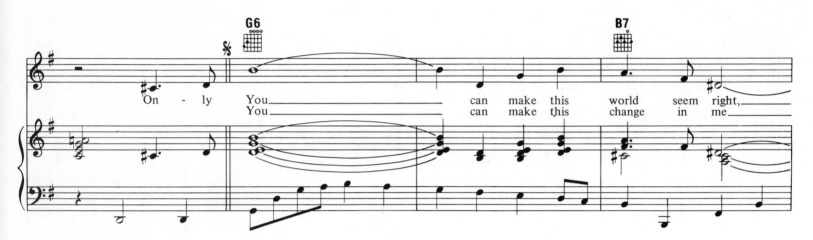

On - ly You   can make this world seem right,
You   can make this change in me

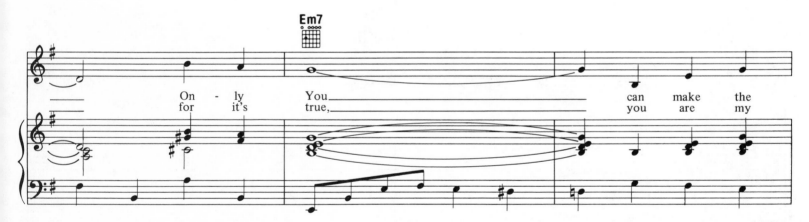

On - ly You   can make the
for it's true,   you are my

To Coda

dark - ness bright.   On - ly You and you, a -
des - ti - ny.   When you hold my hand,   I

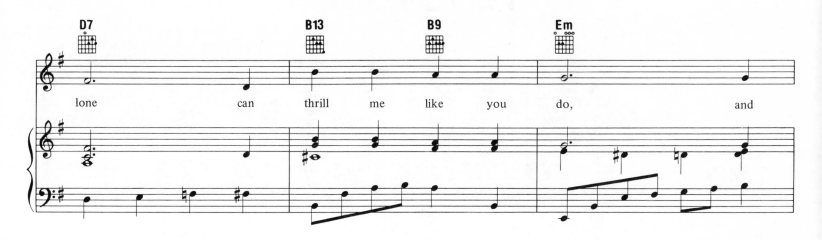

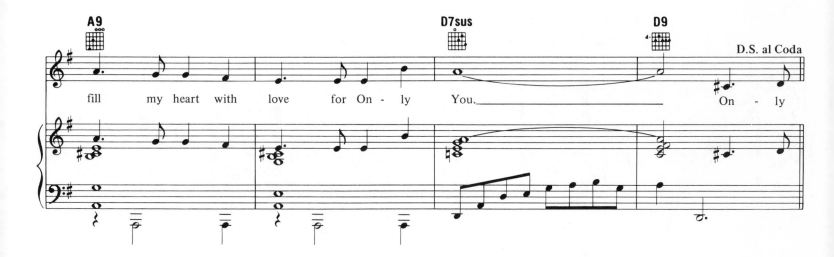

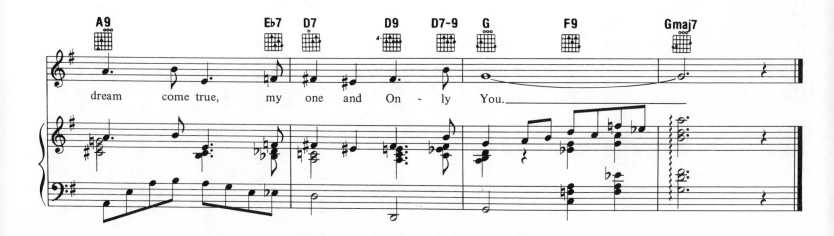

PEGGY SUE

Words and Music by JERRY ALLISON,
NORMAN PETTY and BUDDY HOLLY

Very brightly

mf

If you knew_____ Peg - gy Sue,_____ Then you'd
Peg - gy Sue,_____ Peg - gy Sue,_____ Oh, how

mf

know why I feel blue_____ A - bout Peg - gy,_____
my heart yearns for you,_____ Oh, Pa - heg - gy,_____

'Bout my Peg - gy Sue;_____
My Pa - heg - gy Sue;_____

Oh, well, I love you, gal,___ Yes, I love you, Peg - gy Sue:___

Peg - gy Sue,___

Peg - gy Sue,___ Pret - ty, pret - ty, pret - ty, pret - ty,

Peg - gy Sue,___ Oh, my Peg - gy,___ My

Oh, Peg - gy,_____ My Peg - gy Sue;_

_____ Oh, well, I love you, gal,_

_ Yes, I want you, Peg - gy Sue._____

PLEASE, PLEASE ME

Words and Music by JOHN LENNON
and PAUL McCARTNEY

With a beat

Last night I said these words to my____ girl
You don't need me to show the way____ love

I know you nev-er e-ven try____ girl }
Why do I al-ways have to say____ love }

Come

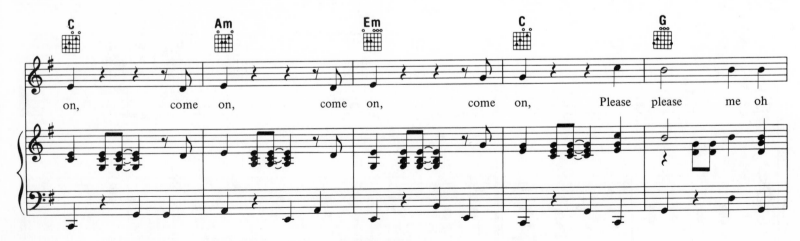

on, come on, come on, come on, Please please me oh

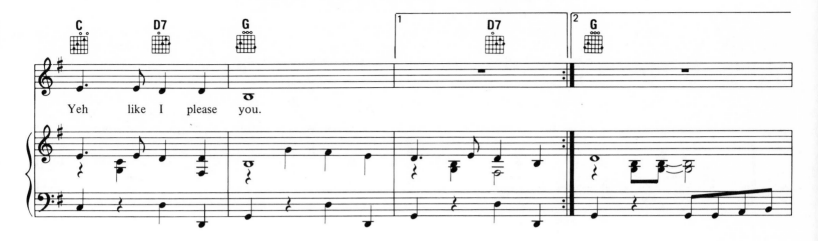

Yeh   like I please   you.

I don't want to sound com - plain - ing But you know there's al - ways rain in my_____ heart.

I do all the pleas - ing with you It's so hard to rea - son with

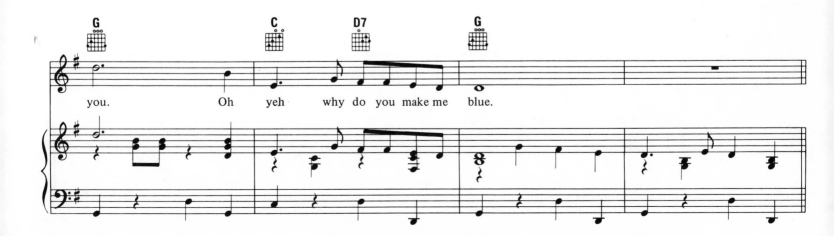

you.   Oh   yeh   why do you make me blue.

Last night I said these words to my _____ girl,

I know you nev - er e - ven try _____ girl   Come on,   come

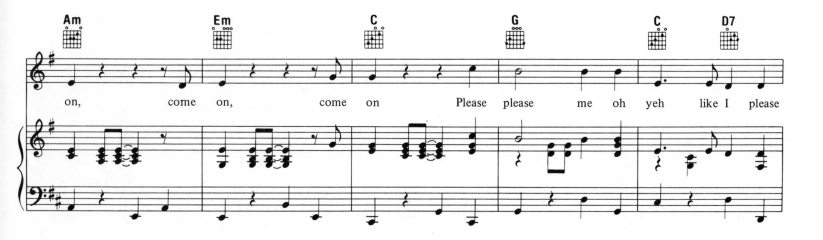

on,   come on,   come on   Please please me oh yeh like I please

you.   you. _____

PUPPY LOVE

Moderately slow

Words and Music by PAUL ANKA

And they called it pup-py love, _____ Oh, I guess they'll nev-er

know, how a young heart real-ly feels, _____

and ___ why I love her so. ___ And they called it pup-py

POISON IVY

Words and Music by JERRY LEIBER
and MIKE STOLLER

PRIMROSE LANE

Words and Music by
WAYNE SHANKLIN and GEORGE CALLENDER

PUT YOUR HEAD ON MY SHOULDER

Words and Music by PAUL ANKA

Just a kiss good-night, May - be You and I will fall in love.

Peo - ple say that love's a game, a game you just can't win.

If there's a way I'll find it some-day, And then this fool will rush

in. Put your head on my should - er, Whis-per in my ear,

READY TEDDY

Up tempo rock

Words and Music by JOHN MARASCALCO
and ROBERT BLACKWELL

Read-y, set, go, man, go, I got a gal that I love so. I'm

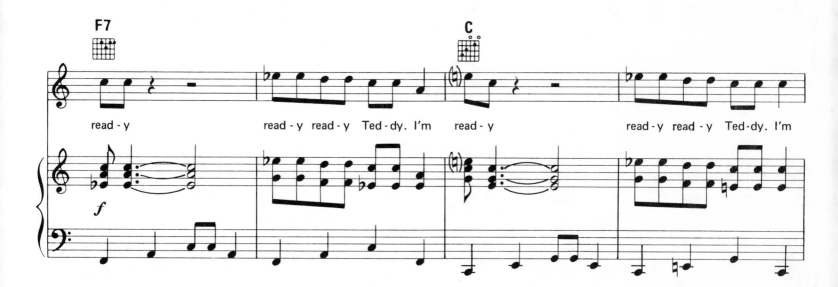

read-y read-y ready Ted-dy. I'm read-y read-y ready Ted-dy. I'm

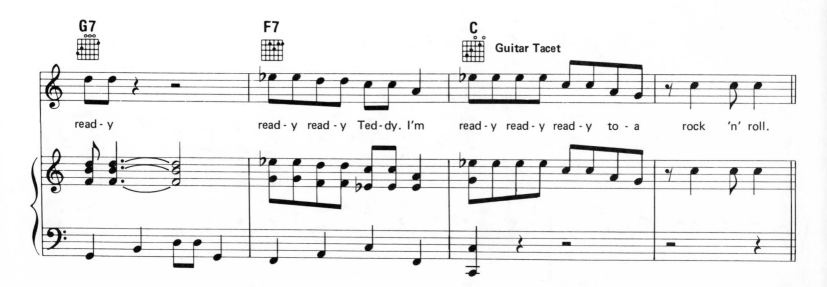

read-y read-y ready Ted-dy. I'm read-y ready ready to-a rock 'n' roll.

REELIN' AND ROCKIN'

Medium shuffle

Words and Music by CHUCK BERRY

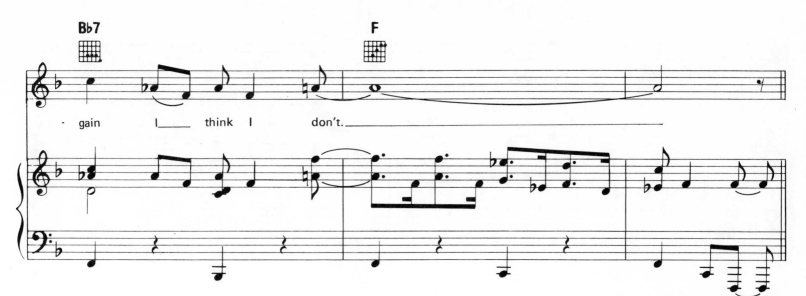

Bb7 **F**

-gain I____ think I don't._____

F

(1 to 10)Well, I____ looked at my watch,
(1.) it was nine_____ twen-ty one,____ 'Twas at a
(2.) it was nine_____ thir-ty two,____ There's noth-in'
(3.) it was nine_____ for-ty three,____ And ev-'ry
(4.) it was nine_____ fif-ty four,____ I said,____
(5.) it was ten_____ o'-five,____ But I'm a
(6.) it was ten_____ twen-ty six,____ I
(7.) it was ten_____ twen-ty eight,_____ I
(8.) it was ten_____ twen-ty nine,____ I had to
(9.) and to my_____ sur-prise_____ I was
(10.)and it was_____ time to go,_____ The

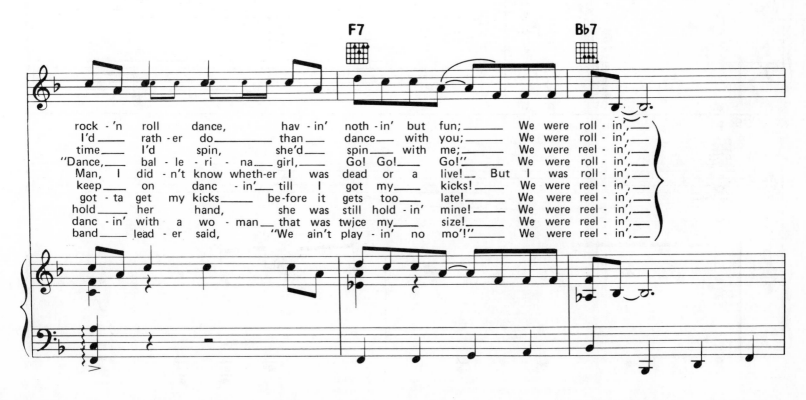

F7 **Bb7**

rock-'n roll dance, hav-in' noth-in' but fun;____ We were roll-in',____
I'd____ rath-er do_____ than____ dance____ with you;____ We were roll-in',____
time____ I'd spin, she'd____ spin____ with me;____ We were reel-in',____
"Dance,____ bal-le-ri-na____ girl,____ Go! Go!____ Go!"____ We were roll-in',____
Man, I did-n't know wheth-er I was dead or a live!____ But I was roll-in',____
keep____ on danc-in' till I got my____ kicks!____ We were reel-in',____
got-ta get my kicks be-fore it gets too____ late!____ We were reel-in',____
hold____ her hand, she was still hold-in' mine!____ We were reel-in',____
danc-in' with a wo-man____ that was twice my____ size!____ We were reel-in',____
band____ lead-er said, "We ain't play-in' no mo'!"____ We were reel-in',____

Reel - in' and a rock - in', _____

We were reel - in' and a rock - in' and roll -

- in 'till the break of dawn. ___

Well, I

Well, I

RETURN TO SENDER

Words and Music by OTIS BLACKWELL
and WINFIELD SCOTT

ad - dress un - known.　　No such num - ber,

no such zone.　　We had a quar - rel,

a lov - er's spat.　　I write I'm sor - ry but my

let - ter keeps com - ing back.　　zone.　　This time I'm gon - na

ROCK AND ROLL MUSIC

Words and Music by CHUCK BERRY

ROCK AROUND THE CLOCK

By MAX C. FREEDMAN
and JIMMY DeKNIGHT

One, two, three o'-clock, four o'-clock rock,

five, six, sev-en o'-clock, eight o'-clock rock, Nine, ten, e-lev-en o'-clock,

twelve o'-clock rock, We're gon-na rock a-round the clock to-night.___

ROLL OVER BEETHOVEN

Words and Music by CHUCK BERRY

Solid rock beat

Well I'm a - write a lit-tle let-ter, gon-na mail it to my lo-cal D. J.

Yes, it's a jump-in' lit-tle rec-ord I want___ my jock-ey to play;

roll o - ver Bee-tho-ven, I got-ta hear it a-gain to-day.___

RUBY BABY

Words and Music by JERRY LEIBER
and MIKE STOLLER

I love a girl and a Ru - by is her name.__ This
Each time I see you,__ ba - by, my heart cries.__ Tell yuh,

girl don't__ love me but I love her just the same.__
I'm gon - na steal__ you a - way from all those guys.__

Ru - by, Ru - by, how I want yuh; like a ghost 'I'm a gon - na haunt yuh.
From the hap - py day I met yuh I made a bet that I was gon - na get yuh.

When this girl looks at me she just sets my heart a-flame.__

Got some hug-gin' and kiss-es too, yeah, and I'm gon-na give them-a all to you. Now lis-ten,

Ru-by, Ru-by, when will you be mine? Ru-by, Ru-by,

when will you be mine?_____

SAD MOVIES
(MAKE ME CRY)

By J.D. LOUDERMILK

SAVE THE LAST DANCE FOR ME

Words and Music by DOC POMUS
and MORT SHUMAN

SHAKE, RATTLE AND ROLL

Words and Music by CHARLES CALHOUN

Moderately Bright

VERSE

Get out ___ from that kitch-en and rat-tle those pots and pans, ___

Get out ___ from that kitch-en and rat-tle those pots and pans. ___

look so warm, ___ but your heart is cold ___ as ice. ___

Verse 3

I'm like a one-eyed cat, ___ peep-in' in a sea-food store, ___

I'm like a one-eyed cat, ___

peep-in' in a sea-food store; ___ I can look at you, ___ tell you

SCHOOL DAY
(RING! RING! GOES THE BELL)

Words and Music by CHUCK BERRY

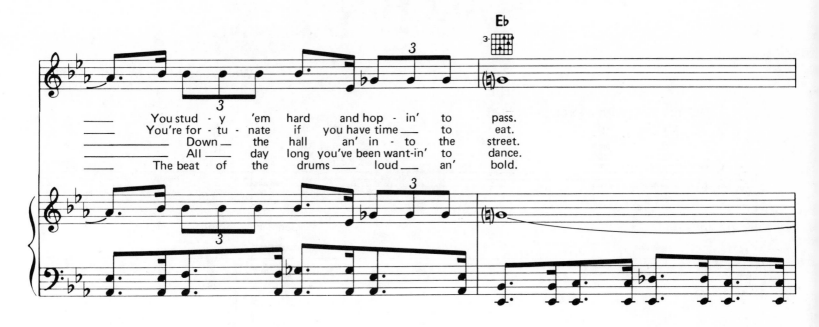

You stud - y 'em hard and hop - in' to pass.
You're for - tu - nate if you have time ___ to eat.
Down ___ the hall an' in - to the street.
The beat of the drums ___ loud ___ an' bold.

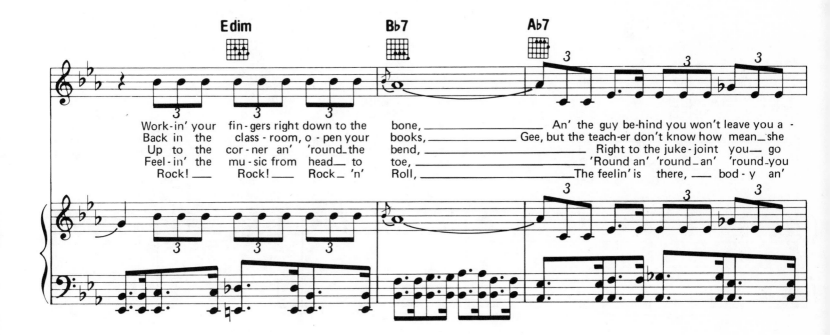

Work - in' your fin - gers right down to the bone, ___ An' the guy be - hind you won't leave you a -
Back in the class - room, o - pen your books, ___ Gee, but the teach - er don't know how mean ___ she
Up to the cor - ner an' 'round the bend, ___ Right to the juke - joint you ___ go
Feel - in' the mu - sic from head ___ to toe, ___ 'Round an' 'round ___ an' 'round ___ you
Rock! ___ Rock! ___ Rock ___ 'n' Roll, ___ The feelin' is there, ___ bod - y an'

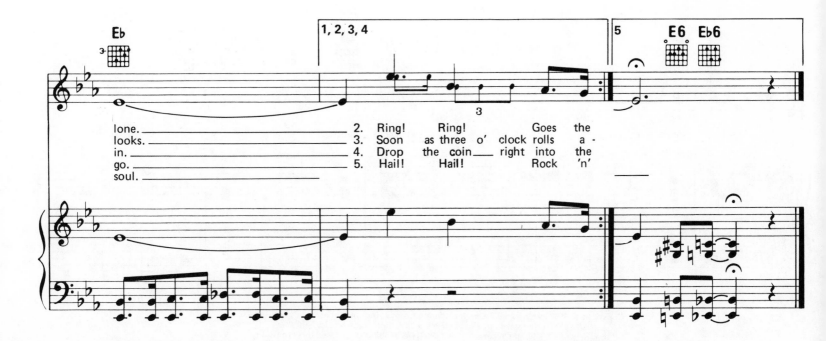

lone. ___ 2. Ring! Ring! Goes the
looks. ___ 3. Soon as three o' clock rolls a -
in. ___ 4. Drop the coin ___ right into the
go. ___ 5. Hail! Hail! Rock 'n'
soul.

Searchin'

Words and Music by JERRY LEIBER
and MIKE STOLLER

SH-BOOM
(LIFE COULD BE A DREAM)

Words and Music by JAMES KEYES,
CLAUDE FEASTER, CARL FEASTER,
FLOYD F. McRAE and JAMES EDWARDS

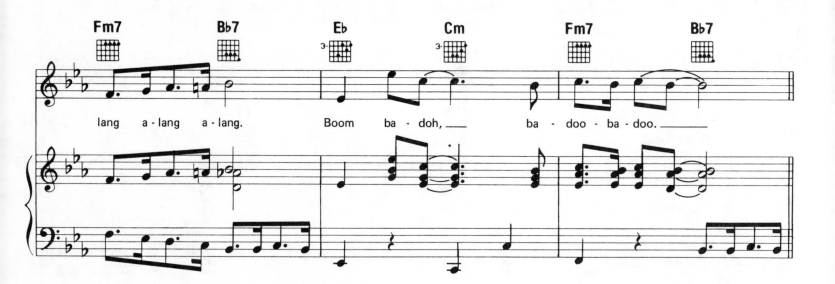

SHE LOVES YOU

Words and Music by JOHN LENNON
and PAUL McCARTNEY

Moderately, with a beat

She loves you, yeh, yeh, yeh,— she loves you, yeh, yeh, yeh,— she

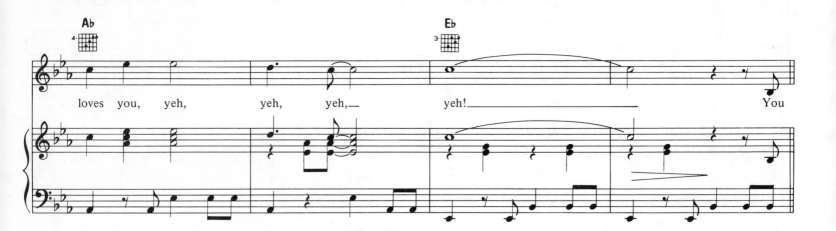

loves you, yeh, yeh, yeh,— yeh!_____ You

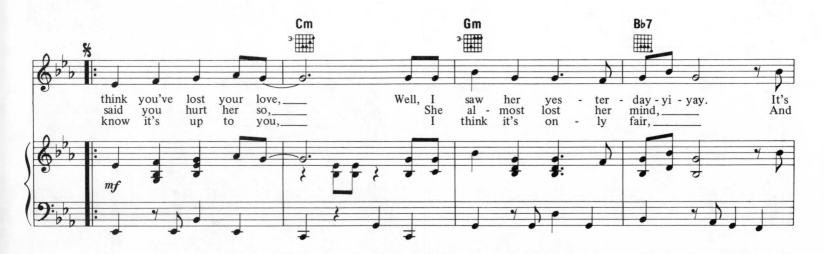

think you've lost your love,___ Well, I saw her yes - ter - day - yi - yay. It's
said you hurt her so,___ She al - most lost her mind,___ And
know it's up to you,___ I think it's on - ly fair,___

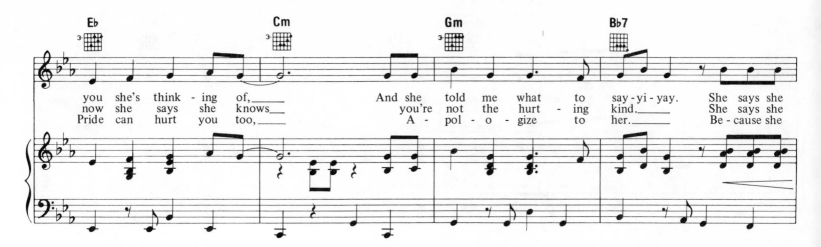

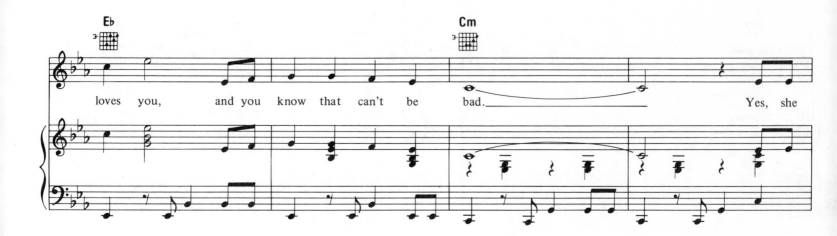

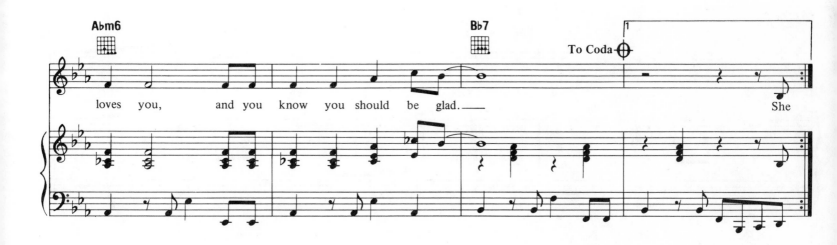

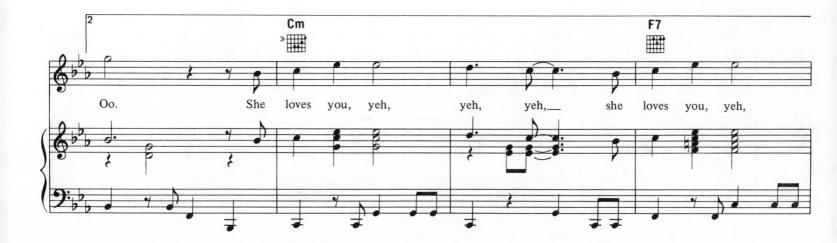

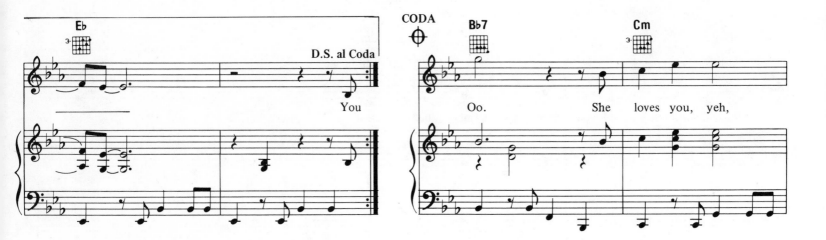

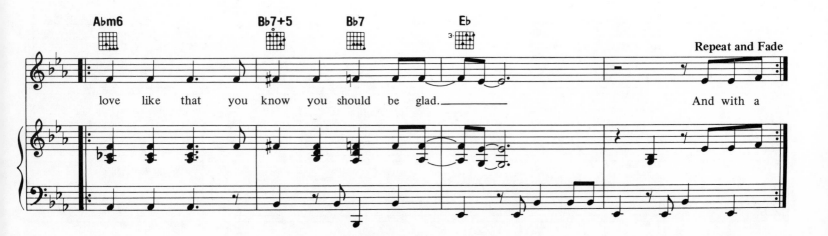

SINCE I MET YOU BABY

Words and Music by
IVORY JOE HUNTER

Slow Blues

Refrain

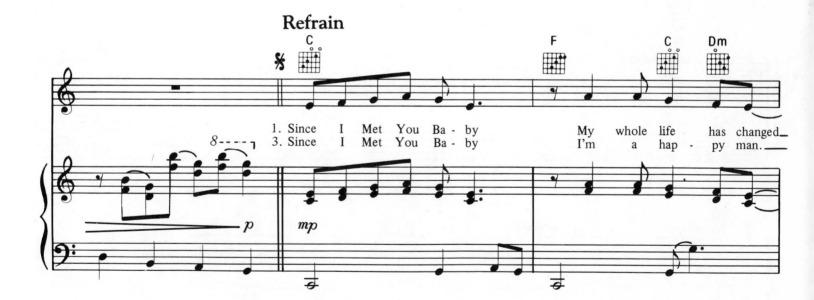

1. Since I Met You Ba - by My whole life has changed
3. Since I Met You Ba - by I'm a hap - py man.

Refrain

2. I don't need no-bod-y to tell my trou-bles to,_____ I don't need no-bod-y to tell my trou-bles to,_____ 'Cause Since I Met You Ba-by all I need is you._____

SILHOUETTES

Words and Music by FRANK C. SLAY JR.
and BOB CREWE

Took a walk and passed your house late last night, All the shades were pulled and drawn 'way down tight; From with-in a dim light cast two sil-hou-ettes on the shade, Oh what a love-ly cou-ple they made. __

Put {his/her} arms a-round your waist, held you tight, kiss-es I could al-most taste in the night, Won-dered why I'm not the {guy/girl} whose sil-hou-ette's on the shade I could-n't hide the tears in my eyes Ah,

SIXTEEN CANDLES

Words and Music by LUTHER DIXON
and ALLYSON R. KHENT

SIXTEEN REASONS
(WHY I LOVE YOU)

Words and Music by BILL & DOREE POST

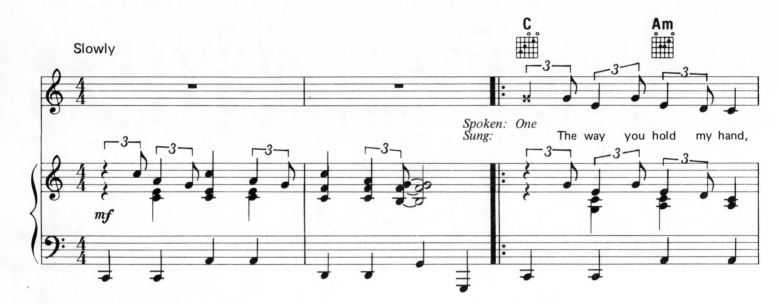

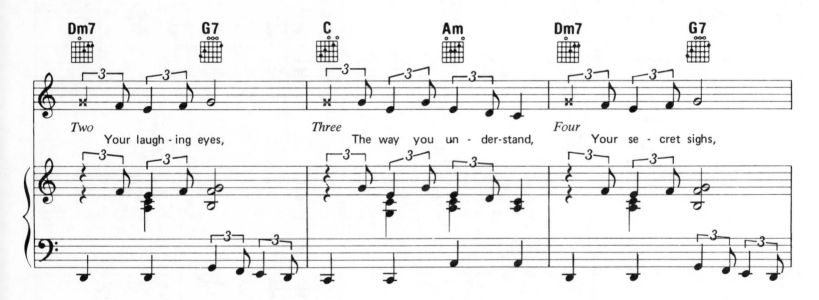

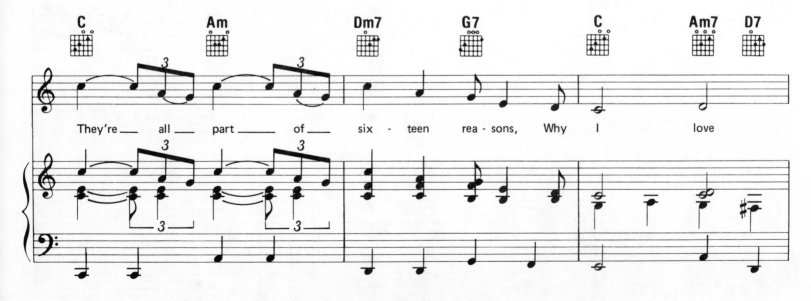

STAND BY ME

Words and Music by BEN E. KING,
MIKE STOLLER and JERRY LEIBER

When the night _____ has come and the land is dark And the moon _____ is the on-ly _____ light we'll see, No, I won't be a-fraid, no _____ I_

SPANISH HARLEM

Words and Music by
JERRY LEIBER and PHIL SPECTOR

Moderately

There is a rose in Span-ish Har-lem,_____

A red rose up in Span-ish Har-lem,_____ It is a
With eyes as

spec-ial one___ It's nev-er seen the sun.___ It on-ly comes out when the moon is on the
black as coal___ that look down in my soul,___ And start a fire___ there and then I lose con-

run and all the stars are gleam - ing,_____ It's grow - ing
trol, I have to beg your par - don,_____ I'm going to

in the street right up thru the con - crete but soft and sweet_ and dream - ing._____
pick that rose_ and watch

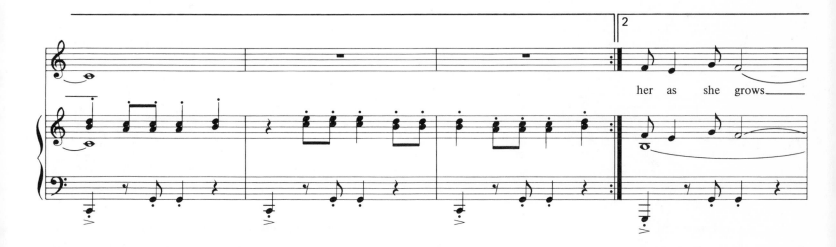

her as she grows_____ to

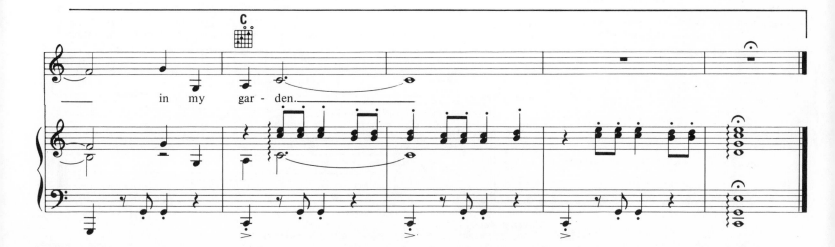

in my gar - den._____

SURFIN' U.S.A.

Music by CHUCK BERRY
Lyric by BRIAN WILSON

Solid shuffle beat

If ev-'ry-bod-y had an o cean a-cross the U. S. A.
(We'll all be plan-nin' out a) route we're gon-na take real soon

Then ev-'ry-bod-y'd be surf-in'
We're wax-in' down our surf boards

like Cal-i-for-ni-a. You'd see them wear-in' their
we can't wait for June. We'll all be gone for the

TEARS ON MY PILLOW

Words and Music by SYLVESTOR BRADFORD
and AL LEWIS

SUSIE Q

Words and Music by D. HAWKINS,
S.J. LEWIS and E. BROADWATER

Medium solid rock beat

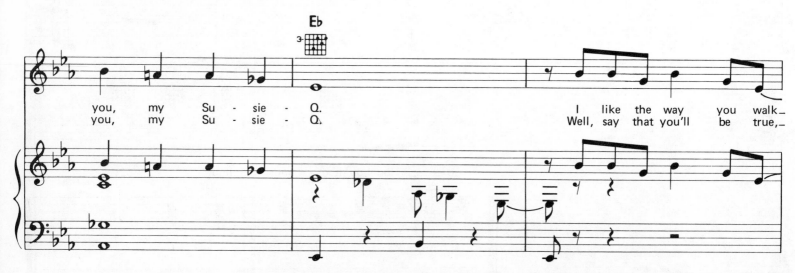

SUSPICION

Words and Music by DOC POMUS
and MORT SHUMAN

Do you speak the same words to some - one else___ when I'm not there?
Why am I so doubt - ful when - ev - er you___ are out of sight?
May - be I'm sus - pi - cious 'cause true love is___ so hard to find.

Sus -

pi - cion___ tor - ments my heart.___ Sus - pi - cion___ keeps us a - part.___ Sus -

pi - cion,___ why tor - ture me!___

me!___ Why tor - ture me!___

SWEET LITTLE SIXTEEN

Words and Music by CHUCK BERRY

(LET ME BE YOUR)
TEDDY BEAR

Words and Music by KAL MANN
and BERNIE LOWE

Medium Bright Rock

Chorus

1. Ba - by, let me be your lov - in' Ted - dy
2. Ba - by, let me be a - round you ev - 'ry

Bear.
night.

Put a chain a - round my neck ___ and
Run your fin - gers through my hair ___ and

A TEENAGER IN LOVE

Moderately slow

Words and Music by DOC POMUS
and MORT SHUMAN

Each time we have a quar-rel it al-most breaks my heart.
One day I feel so hap-py; next day I feel so sad.

'Cause I am so a-fraid that we will have to part.
I guess I'll learn to take the good___ with the bad.

Each night I ask the stars up a-bove:

And if you should say good-bye, I'll still go on lov-ing you.

Each night I ask the stars up a-bove:

Guitar Tacet

Why must I be a teen-ag-er in love, in

1 love?

2 love?

THAT'LL BE THE DAY

Words and Music by NORMAN PETTY,
BUDDY HOLLY and JERRY ALLISON

Moderately with a Beat

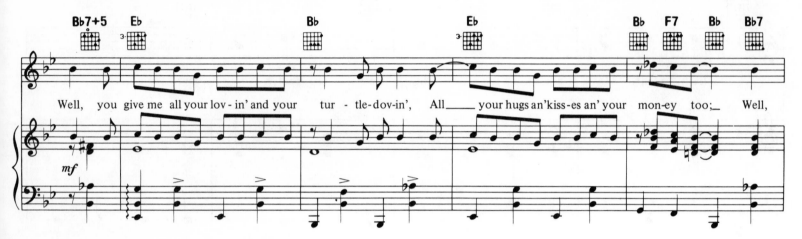

Well, you give me all your lov-in' and your tur-tle-dov-in', All___ your hugs an' kiss-es an' your mon-ey too; Well,

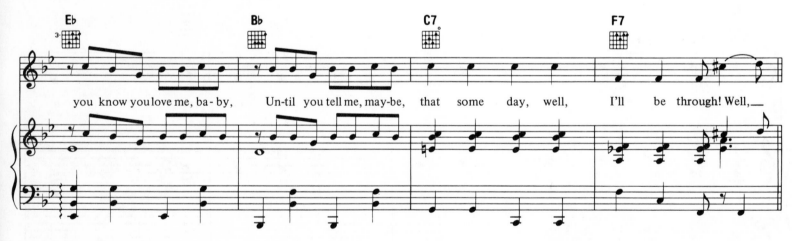

you know you love me, ba-by, Un-til you tell me, may-be, that some day, well, I'll be through! Well,___

That-'ll Be The Day, when you say, good-bye, Yes,___ That-'ll Be The Day, when

you make me cry, Ah, you say you're gon-na leave, you know it's a lie,___ 'cause

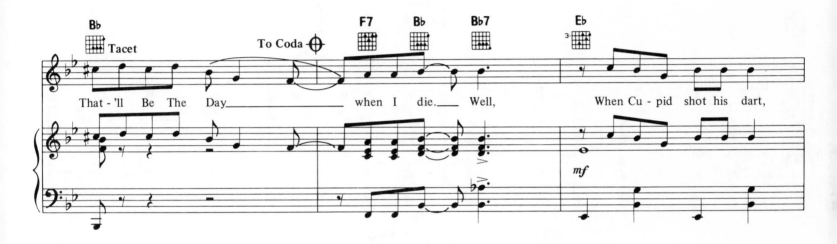

That-'ll Be The Day___ when I die.___ Well, When Cu-pid shot his dart,

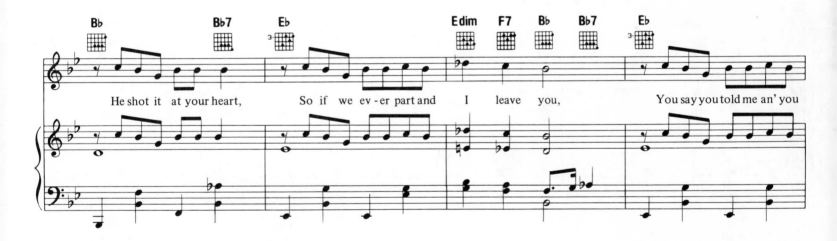

He shot it at your heart, So if we ev-er part and I leave you, You say you told me an' you

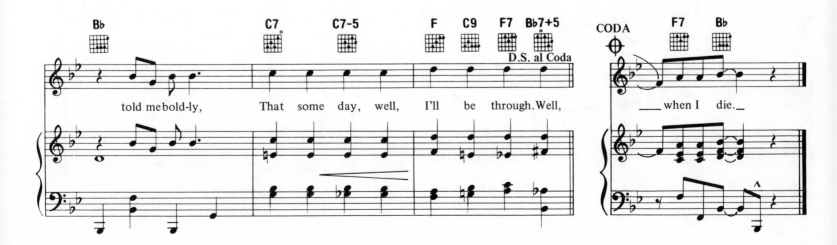

told me bold-ly, That some day, well, I'll be through. Well, ___ when I die.___

TOBACCO ROAD

Moderately with a back beat

Words and Music by JOHN D. LOUDERMILK

TRUE LOVE WAYS

Words and Music by NORMAN PETTY
and BUDDY HOLLY

Slowly

Just you know

why, why you and I will by and

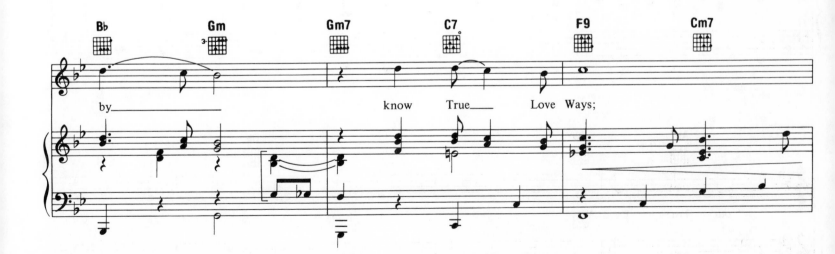

by_____ know True____ Love Ways;

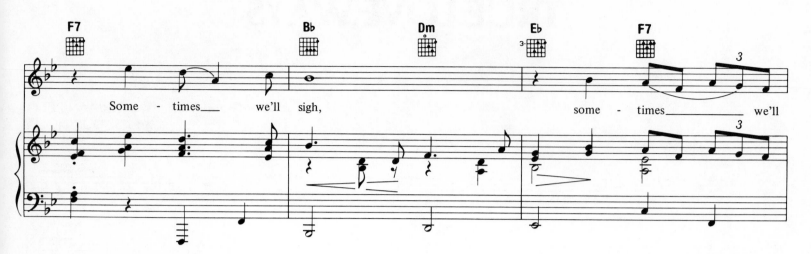

Some - times___ we'll sigh, some - times_____ we'll

cry, And we'll know why, just you ___ and

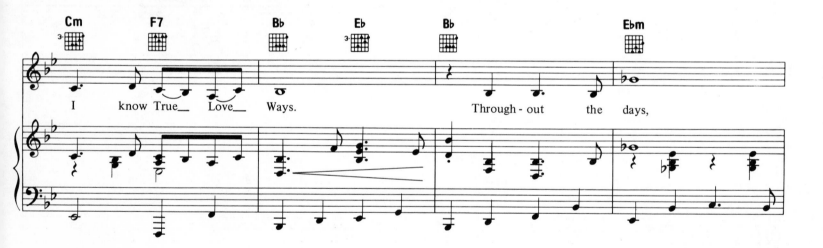

I know True__ Love__ Ways. Through - out the days,

our True Love Ways will bring us joys to share with

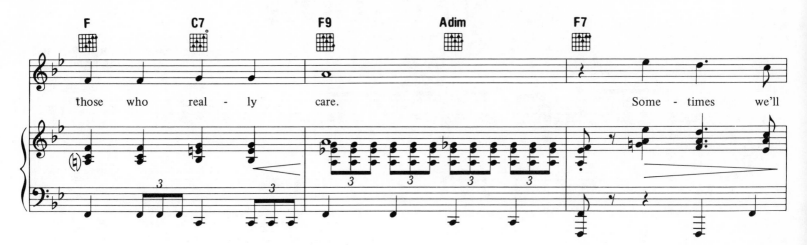

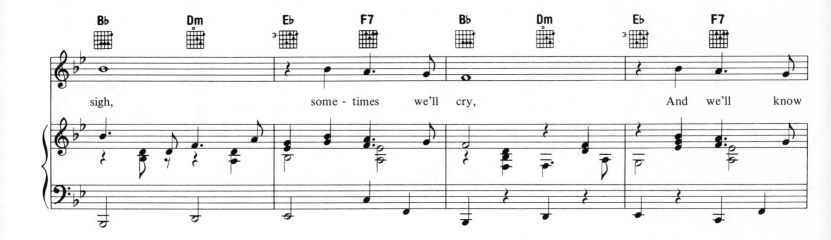

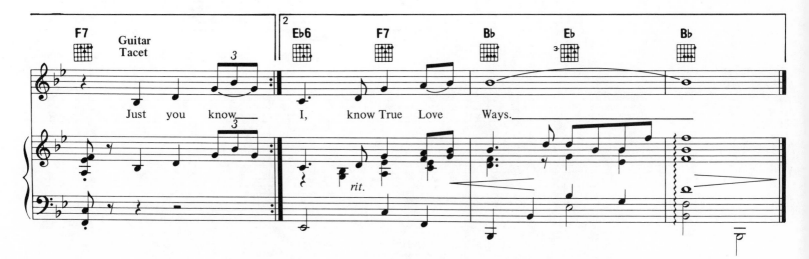

TURN ME LOOSE

Words and Music by DOC POMUS
and MORT SHUMAN

Turn me loose, turn me loose, I say, ___ This is the first time I ev - er

felt this way. Gon - na get a thou - sand kicks, gon - na kiss a thou - sand chicks, So turn me

loose. Turn me loose, turn me

WAKE UP, LITTLE SUSIE

By BOUDLEAUX BRYANT
& FELICE BRYANT

Rock Tempo

Wake Up, Lit - tle Su - sie,___ wake up.

We've both been sound a - sleep,___ Wake Up,___ Lit - tle Sus - ie and

The mov - ie was-n't so hot,___ It did - n't have much of a

weep. The mov - ie's o - ver it's four o - clock___ and we're in trou - ble

plot. We fell a - sleep, and our goose is cooked,___ our rep - u - ta - tion is

TWO FACES HAVE I

Words and Music by LOU SACCO
and TWYLA HERBERT

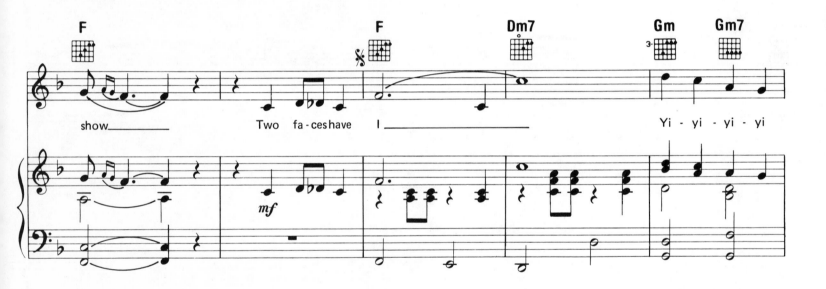

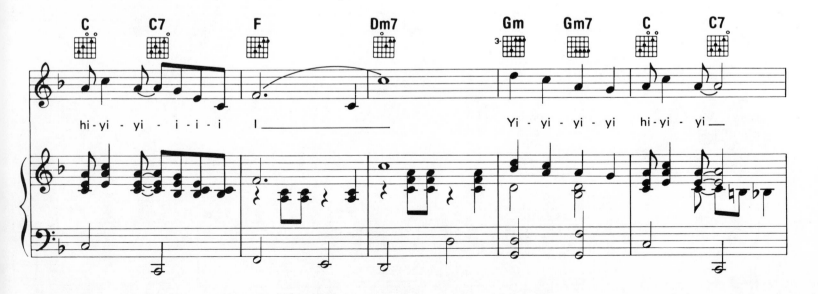

WEAR MY RING AROUND YOUR NECK

Words and Music by BERT CARROLL,
RUSSELL MOODY and MARILYN SHACK

Bright tempo

WHAT'S YOUR NAME?

Words and Music by CLAUDE JOHNSON

Ma - ry or Sue? What's your name? Do I stand a _____ chance with you? It's so

hard to find a per - son - al - i - ty with charms like yours for me. Ooh - wee, ___ ooh - wee, ___ ooh -

wee. What's your wee. What's your name, what's your

name, what's your name? _____

WHAT'D I SAY

Medium Bounce

Words and Music by RAY CHARLES

Hey, Ma - ma don't you treat me wrong,—
See the girl __ with the dia - mond ring,—
Tell your Ma - ma_____ tell your Pa, —

Come and love me all night long.
She knows__ how to twist that thing.
I'm gon - na ship you back to Ar - kan - sas.

Oh, _____ oh, ___ Hey,
Oh, _____ oh, ___ Hey,
Oh, _____ yes ___ You don't do

YAKETY-YAK

Words and Music by JERRY LEIBER
and MIKE STOLLER

1. Take out the pa - pers and the trash,
2. (Just fin - ish clean - ing up your) room.
3. (You just put on your coat and) hat.
4. (Don't you give me no dirt - y) looks.

or you don't get no spend - ing cash.
Let's see that dust fly with that broom.
And walk your - self to the laun - dry - mat.
Your fa - ther's hip; he knows what cooks.

WHO DO YOU LOVE

Solid beat

Words and Music by ELLAS McDANIEL

I walk for-ty sev-en miles of barb wire Use a cob-ra snake for a neck-tie Got a brand new house on the road-side __ Made from rat-tle-snake hide I got a brand new chim-ney made on top Made from a hu-man skull Now

Play 4 times

come on ba-by let's take a lit-tle walk and tell me Who do you love?

Ar-lene took me by the hand,_ she said "Oo-ee, dad-dy, I un-der-stand

Play 3 times

Who do you love?_ Who do you love?"_ The

night was black and the night was blue_ And a-round the cor-ner an ice wa-gon flew, A

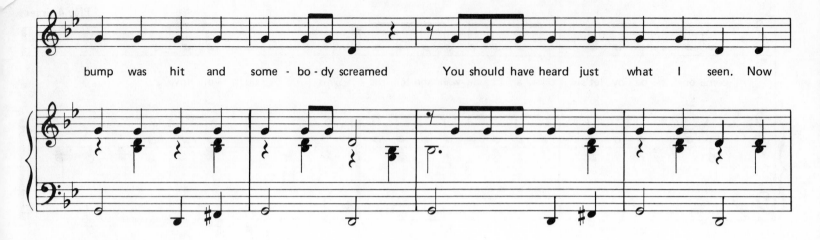

bump was hit and some - bo - dy screamed   You should have heard just   what   I   seen. Now

Play 3 times

who   do   you   love? __   Who   do   you   love? __   I got a

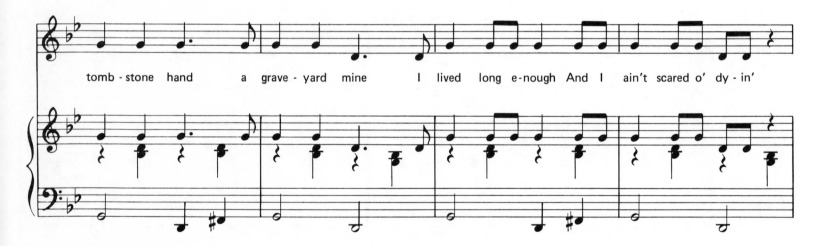

tomb - stone hand   a   grave - yard mine   I   lived   long e - nough And I   ain't scared o' dy - in'

Play 3 times

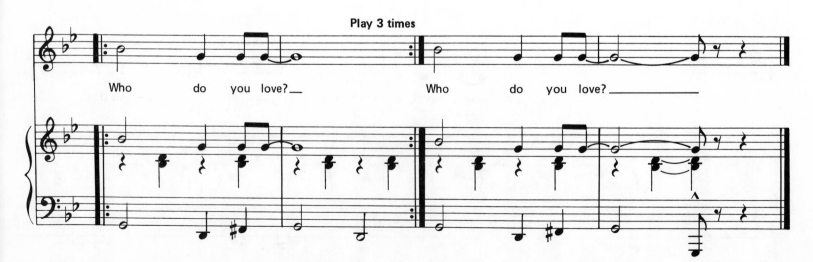

Who   do   you   love? __   Who   do   you   love? _____

YOU CAN'T SIT DOWN

Words and Music by DELECTA CLARK,
CORNELL MULDROW and KAL MANN

Bright Gospel Rock

Hey, pret - ty ba - by, you
When you're on South Street you

can't sit down. ___ Don't you hear the drum - mer thump - in', you
can't sit down. ___ And the band is real - ly boot - in', you

can't sit down, ___ You got to shake it like a cra - zy, you
can't sit down, ___ You hear the hip - py with the back beat you

YOUNG BLOOD

Words and Music by JERRY LEIBER,
MIKE STOLLER and DOC POMUS